Bake Knit Sew
A Recipe and Craft Project Annual

By Evin Bail O'Keeffe

Published by
Anchor and Bee
Cork, Ireland

Photography by: Evin Bail O'Keeffe
Fin McAteer & Victor Sullivan

Published in 2014 by Anchor and Bee
Cork City, County Cork, Republic of Ireland

anchorandbee.com

A CIP catalogue record for this book is available from the British Library.

ISBN 978-1-910567-00-5

Designer: Evin Bail O'Keeffe
Knitting Pattern Editor: Suzanne McEndoo
Recipe Editor: Kristin Jensen
Photographers: Evin Bail O'Keeffe, Fin McAteer, and Victor Sullivan
Book Design: Evin Bail O'Keeffe and Fin McAteer
Proofreaders: William G. Bail, Marseille Bunk, Arlene Cooke,
               Tim Nixon, Carlota Sage, and Victor Sullivan

Contents

To my family and friends who are like family. You mean more to me than you know.

To all those who share my enthusiasm for following dreams and letting creativity take over the corners of our lives.

Introduction

Hi, thanks for stopping by.

This book has been a labor of love. As any of my EvinOK.com blog readers know, I have a passion for knitting and baking, and relish in sharing it. I hope this book helps to inspire you to be as creative as you can be. In this age of mass consumption and branding, there is magic in being able to create something unique and special. Something all your own, from the heart. As gifts, handmade objects can delight and have so much more meaning then store bought items. For as long as I've knitted, I've found immense joy in crafting one-of-a-kind baby gifts for my friends. There is something that warms from the inside out when someone knows they are cherished enough to be given something made with all your heart and enthusiasm. Whether it is knit, sewn, or baked, it's from you and that's what matters.

Combining baking recipes, knitting patterns, and sewing projects can be tricky unless they tie together in some way. For me, the seasons and months are the unifying bond for each pair. The recipes and patterns/projects are thematically related by having a situational relationship – intuitively, they seem to naturally go together. Whenever possible, the ingredients and materials are seasonally appropriate. Warm wool and hearty pies in autumn and winter, while summer enjoys crisp cottons and fresh fruit.

The recipes within these pages are well-tested and well-loved. Some have been perfected by generations of my family. Years ago, a worn enamelware box found its way into my hands but, at the time, I didn't know it was actually a treasure box. It held all my Grandma's recipes, which included her mother's and her mother's mother's favorite recipes. It is difficult to put into words how dearly I cherish my family recipes. That having been said, I enjoy adapting, updating, and playing with the recipes for new modern variations. Some of them have found their way into this volume just for you!

The knitting patterns and sewing projects are items I designed with a hefty dose of practicality and comfort in mind. The materials really bring out the natural beauty of each project and are also where you can flex your own personality the most. Don't hesitate to make each piece an example of your creativity with custom fabric combinations or wild colors. These projects are a detailed jumping off point for you to create your own hand-crafted treasures.

I hope you enjoy this book and have as much fun trying out its contents as I had making it. Join me, @FreckledPast on Twitter and Instagram as I continue to bake, knit, sew, travel, and share the process.

XOXO
Evin

P.S. And visit my website/blog: evinok.com for more recipes and projects.

Snyder Family Pie Crust

This recipe comes from the Pennsylvania Dutch side of my family. Tried and tested over generations, I began adding ground cinnamon to my crust for added flavor and this soon became my go-to shortcrust recipe. For sweet pies and tarts, I prefer ground cinnamon or even ground cardamom, but for savory quiches and tarts, I opt for ground savory, paprika, or Old Bay Seasoning.

1 cup (120g) all-purpose flour
1/2 teaspoon baking powder
1/2 teaspoon ground cinnamon or ground
  cardamom (omit for savory pies)
1/4 teaspoon salt
1/3 cup (75g) very cold butter, cut into
  pea-sized pieces
1/4 cup (50ml) cold whole milk

Makes 1 x 9in (23cm) pie crust

Note:
  If you want to make two crusts, simply double the ingredient quantities.

1. Preheat the oven to 350°F (180°C).

2. In a large mixing bowl, mix the flour, baking powder, cinnamon, and salt together.

3. Cut in the butter without warming the mixture until it resembles breadcrumbs, then gradually add the milk until the pastry just comes together to form a ball. At this point, you can chill it overnight if you are making this ahead of time or if you are working in a warm kitchen.

4. Lightly dust a cold, clean countertop or baking board with flour and roll out the pastry fairly thinly, handling it as little as possible. You should have enough to make one 9in (23cm) single-crust pie. Transfer the rolled-out crust to your pie dish. Trim the excess pastry or crimp the edges to form a decorative edging.

5. To blind bake the crust, place a square of parchment paper over the top of the pastry. Fill with dry rice, or beans, or baking beans. Bake the crust for 30 minutes in the preheated oven. It will be light golden brown. Remove the paper and beans, then return it to the oven for another 5–10 minutes. Remove from the oven and let it rest for 1 hour to cool before adding in your pie filling.

6. Before you pour in the filling, brush the exposed surfaces of the pie crust with some lightly beaten egg yolk. This will keep the crust from getting soggy when you pour the filling in.

7. Follow the recipe for your pie filling, pour into the crust, and bake according to your pie recipe.

Long-tail Cast On

The Long-tail Cast On is versatile, stretchy, and has the strength and appearance of a knitted row as the edge. It is used in this book frequently. For a video tutorial, visit my website: evinok.com

The length of the tail should be determined based on how many stitches you are casting on and what weight yarn and size needles. To estimate tail length, wrap your yarn around the knitting needle as many times as the number of stitches you plan to cast on then add a few inches to that.

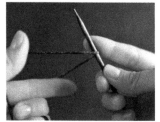

1. To start, hold the yarn as shown above with the tail in front, draping over your thumb and held in the hand. The ball-end of the section of yarn goes down behind your index finger and is held in your hand by your other three fingers. To cast on, drape the yarn over the needle as shown in the first figure, leaving an ample tail. You may also begin with a slipknot, if you prefer.

2. Pull your needle forward to pick up the yarn between the nail and first knuckle of your thumb.
   Pick it up through the side facing your palm.

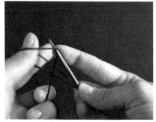

3. Pull the picked up yarn backward over the yarn coming from the back of your thumb.

4. Pick up the yarn being held by your index finger.

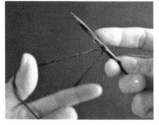

5. Release the yarn from your thumb behind the freshly created first stitch and repeat this process as many times as needed for your project to be cast on.

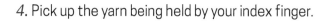

6. The cast on stitches are complete and you may begin your first row.

Icelandic Bind Off

The Icelandic Bind Off is a beautiful completion to a project with a firm yet stretchy edge. For added looseness, go up a needle size for bind off. For a video tutorial, visit my website: evinok.com

1. Knit into the first stitch.

2. Slip the knitted stitch from the right needle back to the left needle purlwise.

3. Through the slipped stitch, go through the second stitch to knit into it.

4. Knit into the second stitch.

5. Slip both stitches off the left needle with the new stitch on your right needle.

6. Repeat steps 2–5 with the remaining stitches until one remains. Trim and slip the remaining yarn tail through the loop to close off and weave in the end as needed for your pattern.

Knitting Glossary

Here are terms and abbreviations used in the patterns of this book.

... - Use of astrixes around a segment of the pattern denotes repetition.

000yd / 000m / 000g - Each knitting pattern has the yarn quantity detailed in this format: yards/meters/grams.

Bind Off - The final row to secure your final of stitches to one another in sequence so they do not unravel. This can add an added texture and beauty as well.

Block - After a knitted garment or item is complete, sometimes the stitches may be uneven or edges may roll. Blocking trains the stitches to lay flat or take on a shape, such as a tea cosy, using steam or moisture followed by drying time in a set position. This should not be done on ribbing or other stitches requiring a retention of stretch. Lace knitting is especially transformative when blocked. For a blocking tutorial, visit my website: evinok.com

Cast On - The first row of stitches to secure the edge of your knitted project as you begin. For a hat, this is often the brim edge.

Chart - A visual represenatation of the stitches in a pattern.

Gauge - How many stitches and rows in a 4-by-4-inch section of knitted material are needed to create the project in the desired size and stitch density. Can be measured in stockinette or pattern stitches. If the pattern doesn't specify a pattern for the gauge swatch, use stockinette stitch

In the round - A pattern knit "In the round" is knit in a continuous circle rather than back and forth. This gives a seamless tube of knitting and is used for items like hats or cowls.

K2tog - Knit two stitches together at this part of the pattern. This is used as a manner of decreasing stitches, to balance added stitches for a consistent stitch count, or for a design feature.

Knitwise - The right needle slipping into a stitch on the left needle from left to right, as if to knit the stitch.

M1 - Make one increase, aka make one left. Lift the bar between the stitch you just knit and the next stitch, using your left needle by inserting the needle from the front. You now have a loop of yarn sitting over your left needle. Knit into the back of this loop to create the new stitch.

PM or SM - Place a stitch marker (PM) or slip the stitch marker (SM).

Purlwise - The right needle slipping into a stitch on the left needle in a straight opposing direction (from right to left), as if to purl the stitch.

Right side - The outside of the fabric or item. What will show to the world when you wear/use it.

Wrong side - The inside of the fabrc or item. What will not show when you wear/use it.

YO - Yarn over. Move the yarn between the needles as if you were about to purl, then bring it up and over the right needle to the back, ready for the next knit stitch

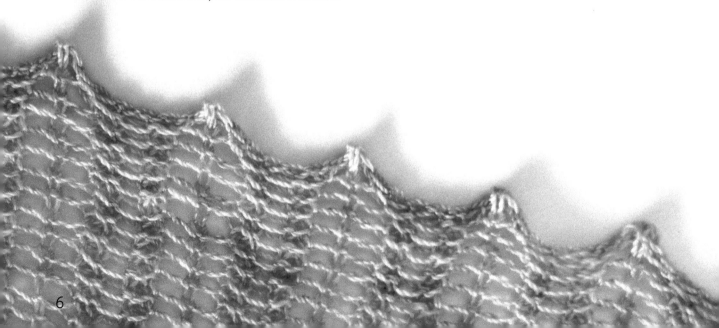

Sewing Glossary

Here is a collection of terms referenced in the projects within this book.

Bias tape - A narrow strip of fabric, cut on the bias, for flexibility and stretchiness. It can be purchased or made. It is usually folded in on two sides and folded over edges/seams for a decorative or strengthening element.

Prewashed fabric - Fabric that is washed and dried as the final item will be so there is no shrinking, puckering, or distrortion of the final item when washed.

Right side - The outside of the fabric or item. What will show to the world when you wear/use it.

Wrong side - The inside of the fabric or item. What will not show when you wear/use it.

Blanket Stitch

The Blanket Stitch can be used functionally to sew layers of fabric together, decoratively to accentuate an edge, or both ways as in the Upcycled Felt Mittens on page 73. For a video tutorial, visit my website: evinok.com

1. Bring the threaded needle up from the bottom, leaving a little tail of thread at the left-most edge of the area you wish to stitch. This is the set-up first stitch. The Blanket Stitch is done by sewing into the fabric from the top, threading through the loop left by the previous stitch carrying over, and pulling the thread through for a neat tight stitch.

2. Repeat this process for the length of your edge.

3. For the final stitch, knot off and weave the remaining ends of the thread into the project edge where it is unseen.

Winter

Mugwump Oatmeal Pie

My childhood was punctuated with winter trips to visit my Southern grandparents. I would pet geckos, soak up sunshine, and eat pie. Oatmeal pie is a Southern treat that originated in a time when pecans were in short supply, so oats were substituted. Grandpa Skipper's nickname for me was Mugwump, an ancient political term that originally meant something akin to "kingpin."

For the crust:
1 cup (100g) crushed shortbread cookies or
    digestive biscuits
1/4 cup (60g) unsalted butter, diced, at room
    temperature

3/4 cups (125g) light brown sugar
1 1/2 cups (375ml) local honey
1/3 cup (75g) butter, at room temperature
2 tablespoons maple syrup
1 teaspoon vanilla extract
1 1/2 tablespoons all-purpose flour
1 teaspoon ground cinnamon
1/4 teaspoon salt

Makes 1 x 9in (23cm) pie for 8 slices

You'll Also Need:
    9in (23cm) round tart or quiche dish

4 eggs
1 cup (80g) raw quick-cook oats
1/4 cup (50ml) cream

1. Blend the cookie crumbs and the unsalted butter together. Press the mixture into a 9in (23cm) round tart or quiche dish. Refrigerate for 30–60 minutes to let the crumb crust set.

2. Preheat the oven to 325°F (160°C).

3. In a large bowl, cream the brown sugar, honey, butter, maple syrup, and vanilla extract together with a hand-held mixer. Stir in the flour, cinnamon, and salt. Set aside.

4. In a mixing bowl, beat the eggs for almost 1 minute, or until they are frothy. Fold the beaten eggs into the butter and sugar mixture. Stir in the oats and cream, then pour the filling into the set crust.

5. Bake for 40 minutes, or until a knife inserted into the center of the pie comes out clean. Cool to room temperature before serving.

Keating Hat

Years ago, I was in need of a simple hat pattern that was loose enough to not crush my hair or even to make way for a ponytail. After a few attempts, my Keating Hat was created. It is a fairly quick knit in the round and, with two size options, quite a thoughtful gift. Using a colorful yarn brightens any day, even the cold and grey days of January.

Materials:
Smudge Yarns Merino DK weight yarn
Small: 126yd / 115m / 63g
Medium: 165yd / 151m / 83g
-or-
Manos del Uruguay Silk Blend
Small: 126yd / 115m / 42g
Medium: 165yd / 151m / 55g
-or-
Similar weight yarn to obtain gauge

Tools:
4.5 mm (US7) circular knitting needles or size needed to obtain gauge
Scissors and needle to weave in ends

Stockinette Gauge:
23sts x 32rows / 4in x 4in

Sizes:
Small (16.5–21.5" at ribbing, 10" top to brim)
Medium (19.5–26" at ribbing, 11" top to brim)

CO 96 (111)

Slip the first cast on stitch to the other needle then begin by K2tog to join in the round (95, 110 stitches).

Repeat *K3, P2* for all stitches for first 14 rows. The tail from the cast on is a reminder where your round begins/ends.

Switch to stockinette. Knit all stitches for 47 rows.

Decrease stitches

For Medium Size Only:

   K9, K2Tog Repeat to end of the row. (100 stitches)

   Knit stockinette for four rows

   K8, K2Tog Repeat to end of the row. (90 stitches)
   Knit stockinette for three rows

For Small Size Only:
   K17, K2Tog Repeat to end of the row. (90 stitches)

Continue decreases for both sizes as follows:

K7, K2Tog Repeat to end of the row. (80 stitches)

13

K6, K2Tog Repeat to end of the row. (70 stitches)

K5, K2Tog Repeat to end of the row. (60 stitches)

K4, K2Tog Repeat to end of the row. (50 stitches)

K3, K2Tog Repeat to end of the row. (40 stitches)

K2, K2Tog Repeat to end of the row. (30 stitches)

K1, K2Tog Repeat to end of the row. (20 stitches)

K2Tog Repeat to end of the row. (10 stitches)

K2Tog Repeat to end of the row. (5 stitches)

Finishing Touches:
Trim the yarn with an arm's length tail and thread it through the remaining stitches, then knot firmly. Weave the end into the crown of hat.

White Chocolate Cheesecake

My grandmother taught me to make cheesecake when I was 11 years old and ever since I've been playing with the recipe to make it a little different. This white chocolate variation is a favorite and with just the right sweetness for you to enjoy with your Valentine – or your friends.

1 cup (100g) crushed cookies (vanilla wafers, gingersnaps, graham crackers, digestive biscuits or shortbread)
1/3 cup (75g) butter, at room temperature
10oz (280g) white chocolate
3 eggs
1lb (450g) cream cheese, at room temperature
3/4 cup (150g) granulated sugar
1 teaspoon vanilla extract

Serves 8

You'll Also Need:
10in (25.5cm) springform pan

1. Preheat the oven to 350°F (180°C). Grease the sides of a 10in (25.5cm) springform pan with butter.

2. Mix the crushed cookies with the softened butter, then press into the bottom of the greased springform pan. Bake for 10 minutes, then let it cool for a few minutes while you make the cheesecake.

3. Put the white chocolate in a large heatproof bowl set over a pot of simmering water (a double boiler), making sure the water does not touch the bottom of the bowl. Allow the chocolate to melt, then remove the bowl from the heat.

4. Blend the melted chocolate, eggs, cream cheese, sugar, and vanilla extract until thoroughly combined. Pour into the prebaked crust.

5. Bake in the preheated oven for 30–45 minutes.

6. Let the cheesecake cool completely to allow it to set before releasing the sides of the pan. Serve in slices.

Cupid's Arrow Cowl

Cowls are the perfect extra layer of warmth that are durable, fairly snag-resistant, and fashionable. The stitch design for this cowl came from my desire for a pattern that works well with a varied colorway or a solid yarn. The chevron design emulates the pointed end of Cupid's arrow.

Materials:
Lucy Neatby Celestial Blue Faced Aran weight yarn or similar weight yarn to obtain gauge
150yd / 137m / 90g

Tools:
5.5mm circular knitting needles
Scissors and needle to weave in ends.

Pattern Gauge:
14 sts x 24 rows / 4in x 4in

Finished Size:
34in circumference
Each pattern repeat adds about one inch in cowl length.

CO 111 using long-tail cast on

Set up Row 1: Slip last stitch to the left needle and K2tog with yarn in front to join in the round.
Knit the remainder of the row. PM

Set up Row 2: *K4, P1, K5* repeat until end of round.

Pattern Row 1: *K3, P1, K1, P1, K4* repeat until end of round.

Pattern Row 2: *K2, P1, K3, P1, K3* repeat until end of round.

Pattern Row 3: *K1, P1, K5, P1, K2* repeat until end of round.

Pattern Row 4: *P1, K7, P1, K1* repeat until end of round.

Pattern Row 5: *K4, P1, K4, P1* repeat until end of round.

Repeat Pattern Rows 1–5 seven to ten times to attain your desired length.

For the final pattern repeat, follow Pattern Rows 1–4 then follow these next three rows before binding off:

End Row 1: *K8, P1* repeat until end of round.

End Row 2: Knit all

Bind off loosely for stretch (Icelandic bind off recommended), and block.

—	I	I	I	I	—	I	I	I	I	I	**5**
I	—	I	I	I	I	I	I	I	I	—	**4**
I	I	—	I	I	I	I	I	—	I	I	**3**
I	I	I	I	—	I	—	I	I	I	I	**2**
I	I	I	I	I	—	I	I	I	I	I	**1**

Symbols
I	knit
—	purl

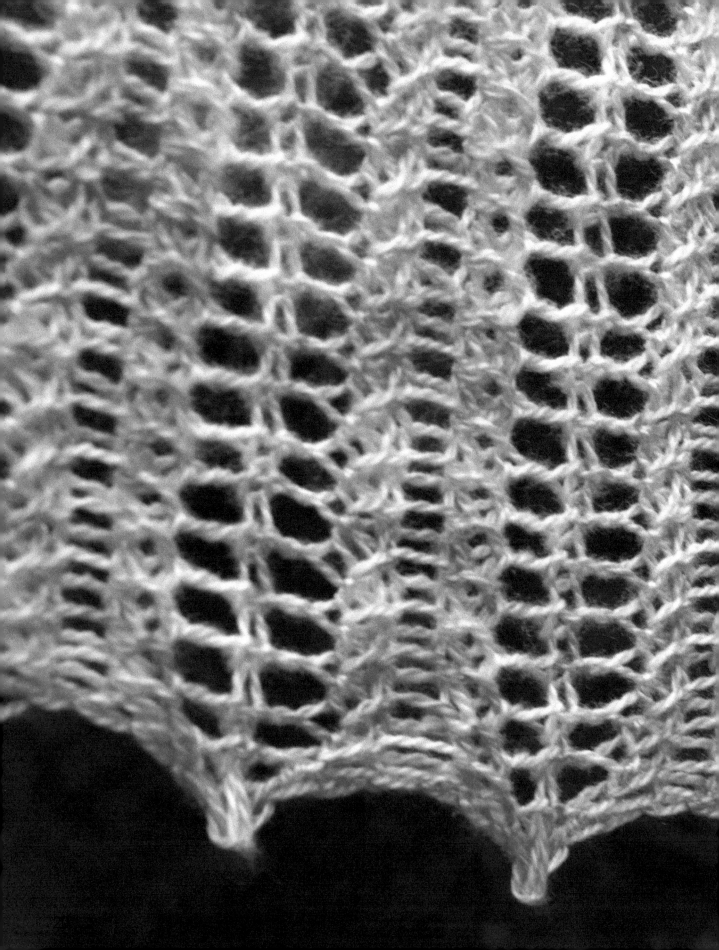

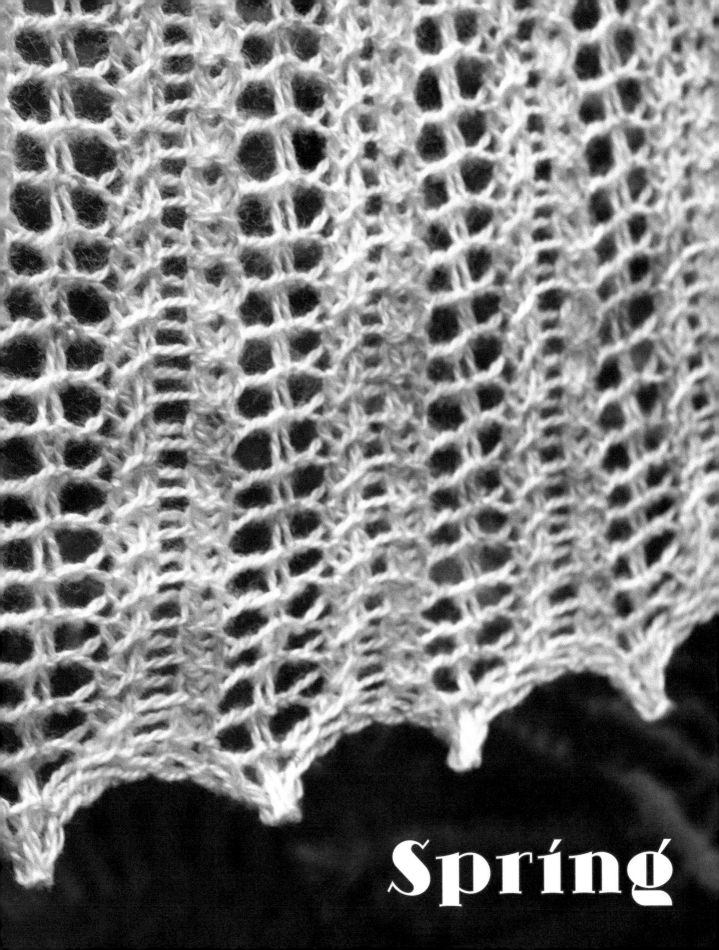

Spring

Lime Poppy Seed Scones

When I moved to Ireland, one of the first surprises was discovering that there are mostly just raisin, plain, or whole-grain scones, unlike the flavorful, fruity ones I grew to love in America. So I set about adapting my great-grandmother's scone recipe to emulate what I missed most. The result is wonderful buttered and drizzled with a heavy spoonful of local honey.

2 cups (250g) self-rising flour
1 tablespoon baking powder
3 tablespoons granulated sugar
2 tablespoons lime zest
1 1/2 tablespoons poppy seeds
pinch of salt
4 tablespoons (60g) butter, chilled and cut
    into dice-sized cubes
3/4 cup (175ml) cream
2 teaspoons lemon extract
2 tablespoons lime juice
1 egg white
2 tablespoons milk

Makes 8 scones

1. Sift the flour and baking powder into a medium bowl. Sprinkle the sugar, lime zest, poppy seeds, and salt over the top, then stir to blend. Refrigerate this flour mixture for 10–30 minutes.

2. Preheat the oven to 425°F (220°C). Grease a baking sheet.

3. Cut in the butter, working quickly to avoid warming the dough too much. Once it's crumbly, pour in the cream and lemon extract, working quickly and handling the dough as little as possible. Pour in the lime juice, then tip the dough out onto a lightly floured surface. Knead the dough lightly, then flatten the dough with the heel of your hand to form a large, flat circle.

4. Cut the large circle into 8 triangular sections, or cut into circles with a scone cutter. Transfer to the greased baking sheet.

5. In a small bowl, lightly beat the egg white and milk together. Brush the tops of the scones with this egg wash (do not brush the sides), then bake for 10–12 minutes.

6. Allow to cool slightly on a wire rack, then serve with butter and jam. These are lovely warm or at room temperature.

Cobblestone Boot Toppers

From October to March, I live in my boots. They protect me from the chill of the wind and transition from jeans to dresses with ease. But I longed for a little insulation to keep wind, rain, or sea spray from sneaking into the boot tops so I whipped up these quick knit boot toppers. They work equally well over fine leather boots or practical rain and sailing all-weather boots.

Materials:
Smudge Yarns Irish Aran weight yarn or similar weight yarn to obtain gauge
Small: 64–97yd / 58–89m / 38–57g
Medium: 72–107yd / 66–98m / 42–63g
Large: 73–112yd / 67–102m / 43–66g
(range depends on number of pattern repeats)

Tools:
5.5mm DPNs or circular knitting needles using magic loop method or size needed to obtain gauge.
Scissors and needle to weave in ends.

Pattern Gauge:
17.0 sts x 24 rows / 4in x 4in, in pattern

Finished Size (Circumference Range):
Small: 9–12in
Medium: 11–15in
Large: 13–17in

CO 40 (48, 56) using long-tail cast on method, join in the round

Rows 1–3: Knit all

Row 4: *K3, P2, K1, P2* repeat five (six, seven, eight) times to complete the round

Row 5: *K3, P1, K1, P1, K1, P1*

Row 6: *K3, P2, K1, P2*

Row 7: *K3, P1, K1, P1, K1, P1*

Rows 8–9: Knit all

Row 10: *P1, K1, P2, K3, P1*

Row 11: *K1, P1, K1, P1, K3, P1*

Row 12: *P1, K1, P2, K3, P1*

Row 13: *K1, P1, K1, P1, K3, P1*

Rows 14–15: Knit all

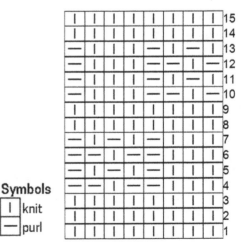

Symbols
I knit
— purl

Repeat rows 4–15 to desired length. Repeat once for boot topper lining, twice or thrice for length to fold over top of boot. Each repeat adds 2.25in to the length of the boot topper and requires 20–30 yards of Aran weight knitting yarn.

Use Icelandic bind off.

Strawberry Mascarpone Tart

When I was freshly engaged, I was writing a weekly recipe column for a newspaper in West Virginia. The town was known for its annual strawberry festival, which inspired so many new adventures in the kitchen with the fresh berries. Unlike some berry tarts, this one is creamy and filling, almost resembling a no-bake cheesecake.

For the crust:
1 cup (100g) crushed shortbread cookies or
    digestive biscuits
1/4 cup (60g) unsalted butter, diced, at room
    temperature

For the filling:
1 egg
1/3 cup (75g) granulated sugar
1/2 cup (40g) quick-cooking plain oats
1/2 cup (175g) seedless strawberry jam
1/4 cup (30g) all-purpose flour
1 tablespoon (15g) salted butter, at room
    temperature

Serves 8

1/8 teaspoon baking powder
4oz (100g) mascarpone cheese, at room
    temperature
9oz (250g) fresh strawberries, hulled and
    sliced
whipped cream, to serve

1. Blend the cookie crumbs and the unsalted butter together. Press the mixture into a 9in (23cm) tart or quiche dish. Refrigerate for 30–60 minutes to let the crumb crust set.

2. Preheat the oven to 325°F (160°C).

3. In a large mixing bowl, beat the egg and sugar together with a hand-held mixer. While continuing to blend with the mixer, add the oats, jam, flour, butter and baking powder. Keep beating until the mixture is smooth.

4. Gently spoon the batter into the set crust. Spread it evenly over the bottom and all the way to the sides of the dish.

5. Bake in the oven for 18–23 minutes. Place on a cooling rack or rest it in a larger dish filled with crushed ice. Once it has cooled to room temperature, it is ready for its next layer.

6. Spread the mascarpone over the cooled cake layer. Arrange the strawberry slices on top of the mascarpone in a decorative circular pattern. Feel free to be creative with this and layer them to add dimension to the tart topping.

7. Cover the tart with plastic wrap to protect it from sediment. Refrigerate it for at least 20 minutes (but no more than 24 hours). Serve with whipped cream.

Falling Petals Lace Shawl

Lace shawls enthral and intimidate me, so I developed this design from my longing to create one that is an ideal first lace knitting project. It reminds me of the end of Spring when the Cherry Blossom trees shed their petals, like nature's confetti. After each row's instructions, the stitch count is noted in parenthesis. For charted instructions for rows 79 to 150, see chart on page 32.

Materials:
Dragonfly Fibres Lace yarn 957yd / 875m / 125g (Springtime in Washington colorway) or or equivalent weight yarn and yardage.

Tools:
3.75mm (US 5) circular needles
58 Stitch markers or 4 drinking straws
Scissors and needle to weave in ends.

Pattern Gauge:
Gauge is not important for this project. The sample was knit in garter stitch at 23sts x 35rows / 4in x 4in, blocked.

Finished Size:
Blocked final size:
35in across at the straight edge;
13in from CO to lace edge straight down;
48in around the crescent lace edge

Notes:
- All even rows from 4–100 are worked in the same manner as Row 2 (Knit all).
- The shawl is semi-circular in shape, with eight increases every four rows.
- After the first six rows, the first and last three stitches are knit.
- In this pattern, there are two types of increases, the make-one increase (m1) and the yarnover (yo). Both of these add stitches to the shawl, but they serve different purposes. The m1 is a hidden increase, sneaking a new stitch onto the needles without being seen. The yo, on the other hand, is the extrovert of the increases. It will leave a little decorative hole in the knitting, which is how we can create beautiful lace patterns in our knitting.
- This pattern uses 5 stitch markers for the body, and 58 stitch markers for the lace edging. If you don't have that many stitch markers, you can use a straw cut into rings. Marker locations are noted every four rows.
- For the plain knit rows and yarnover rows, slip each marker as you come to it.

CO 6 stitches (6)
1. K2, m1, k1, m1, k1, m1, k2 (9)
2. (and all other even rows) Knit all
3. K2, m1, k2, m1, k1, m1, k2, m1, k2 (13)
5. Knit (13)
7. K3, pm, m1, k, m1, k, pm, m1, k, m1, k, pm, m1 , k, m1, k, pm, m1, k, m1, pm, k3 (21)
9. Knit (21)
11. K3, sm, *[m1, k3, m1, k, sm]* four times, k2 (29)
13. Knit (29)
15. K3, sm, *[m1, k5, m1, k, sm]* four times, k2 (37)
17. Knit (37)
19. K3, sm, *[m1, k7, m1, k, sm]* four times, k2 (45)
21. Knit (45)
23. K3, sm, m1, k6, yo, k5, yo, k6, yo, k5, yo, k6, yo, k5, yo, k6, m1, sm, k3 (53)
25. Knit (53)
27. K3, sm, *[m1, k11, m1, k, sm]* four times, k2 (61)
29. Knit (61)
31. K3, sm, m1, k8, yo, k8, yo, k8, yo, k7, yo, k8, yo, k8, yo, k8, m1, sm, k3 (69)

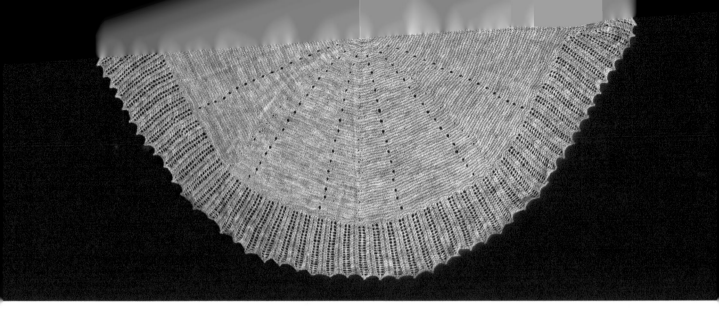

33. Knit (69)
35. K3, sm, *[m1, k15, m1, k, sm]* four times, k2 (77)
37. Knit (77)
39. K3, sm, m1, k10, yo, k10, yo, k10, yo, k11, yo, k10, yo, k10, yo, k10, m1, sm, k3 (85)
41. Knit (85)
43. K3, sm, *[m1, k19, m1, k, sm]* four times, k2 (93)
45. Knit (93)
47. K3, sm, m1, k13, yo, k12, yo, k12, yo, k13, yo, k12, yo, k12, yo, k13, m1, sm, k3 (101)
49. Knit (101)
51. K3, sm, *[m1, k23, m1, k, sm]* four times, k2 (109)
53. Knit (109)
55. K3, sm, m1, k15, yo, k14, yo, k15, yo, k15, yo, k15, yo, k14, yo, k15, m1, sm, k3 (117)
57. Knit (117)
59. K3, sm, *[m1, k27, m1, k, sm]* four times, k2 (125)
61. Knit (125)
63. K3, sm, m1, k17, yo, k17, yo, k17, yo, k17, yo, k17, yo, k17, yo, k17, m1, sm, k3 (133)
65. Knit (133)
67. K3, sm, *[m1, k31, m1, k, sm]* four times, k2 (141)
69. Knit (141)
71. K3, sm, m1, k20, yo, k19, yo, k19, yo, k19, yo, k19, yo, k19, yo, k20, m1, sm, k3 (149)
73. Knit (149)
75. K3, sm, *[m1, k35, m1, k, sm]* four times, k2 (157)
77. Knit (157)
79. K3, sm, m1, k22, yo, k21, yo, k22, yo, k21, yo, k22, yo, k21, yo, k22, m1, sm, k3 (165)
81. Knit (165)
83. K3, sm, *[m1, k39, m1, k, sm]* four times, k2 (173)
85. Knit (173)
87. K3, sm, m1, k24, yo, k24, yo, k24, yo, k23, yo, k24, yo, k24, yo, k24, m1, sm, k3 (181)
89. Knit (181)
91. K3, sm, *[m1, k43, m1, k, sm]* four times, k2 (189)
93. Knit (189)
95. K3, sm, m1, k26, yo, k26, yo, k26, yo, k27, yo, k26, yo, k26, yo, k26, m1, sm, k3 (197)
97. Knit (197)

99. K3, sm, *[m1, k47, m1, k, sm]* four times, k2 (205)
101. Knit (205)
103. K3, sm, m1, k28, yo, k29, yo, k28, yo, k29, yo, k28, yo, k29, yo, k28, m1, sm, k3 (213)
105. Knit (213)
107. K3, sm, *[m1, k51, m1, k, sm]* four times, k2 (221)
109. Knit (221)
111. K3, sm, m1, k30, yo, k31, yo, k31, yo, k31, yo, k31, yo, k31, yo, k30, m1, sm, k3 (229)
113. Knit (229)
115. K3, sm, *[m1, k55, m1, k, sm]* four times, k2 (237)
117. Knit (237)
119. K3, sm, m1, k33, yo, k33, yo, k33, yo, k33, yo, k33, yo, k33, m1, sm, k3 (245)
121. Knit (245)
123. K3, sm, *[m1, k59, m1, k, sm]* four times, k2 (253)
125. Knit (253)
127. K3, sm, m1, k36, yo, k35, yo, k35, yo, k35, yo, k35, yo, k35, yo, k36, m1, sm, k3 (261)
129. Knit (261)
131. K3, sm, *[m1, k63, m1, k, sm]* four times, k2 (269)
133. Knit (269)
135. K3, sm, m1, k38, yo, k37, yo, k38, yo, k37, yo, k38, yo, k37, yo, k38, m1, sm, k3 (277)
137. Knit (277)
139. K3, sm, *[m1, k67, m1, k, sm]* four times, k2 (285)
141. Knit (285)
143. K3, sm, m1, k40, yo, k40, yo, k40, yo, k39, yo, k40, yo, k40, yo, k40, m1, sm, k3 (293)
145. Knit (293)
147. K3, sm, *[m1, k71, m1, k, sm]* four times, k2 (301)
149. Knit (301)
151. K3, sm, m1, k42, yo, k42, yo, k42, yo, k43, yo, k42, yo, k42, yo, k42, m1, sm, k3 (309)
153. Knit (309)
155. K3, sm, *[m1, k75, m1, k, sm]* four times, k2 (317)
157. Knit (317)
158. Knit across as usual, but remove the centre three markers as you go. You should now only have two stitch markers, three stitches in from either end.

Lace Edging:

For rows 13, 21, 27, 35 and 41, you will add two additional stitch markers.

For the last repeat between the *[ ]*, place a new stitch marker where you would otherwise slip the marker.

For charted instructions for lace edging, see chart below. Work the chart three times.

1. K3, sm, m1, k3, m1, k2, pm, *[k2tog, k, yo, k, yo, k, s1kp, pm]*repeat 43 times, k2, m1, k3, m1, sm, k3 (321)

2. (and all other even rows) Knit all.

3. K3, sm, m1, k3, m1, k, yo, k, s1kp, sm, *[k2tog, k, yo, k, yo, k, s1kp, sm]*repeat 43 times, k2tog, k, yo, k, m1, k3, m1, sm, k3 (325)

5. K3, m1, k3, m1, k2tog, yo, k, yo, k, s1kp, sm, *[k2tog, k, yo, k, yo, k, s1kp, sm]*repeat 43 times, k2tog, k, yo, k, yo, s1kp, m1, k3, m1, sm, k3 (329)

7. K3, sm, m1, k3, m1, k, sm, *[k2tog, k, yo, k, yo, k, s1kp, sm]*repeat 45 times, k, m1, k3, m1, sm, k3 (333)

9. K3, sm, m1, k3, m1, yo, k, s1kp, sm, *[k2tog, k, yo, k, yo, k, s1kp, sm]*repeat 45 times, k2tog, k, yo, m1, k3, m1, sm, k3 (337)

11. K3, sm, m1, k3, m1, k2, yo, k, s1kp, sm, *[k2tog, k, yo, k, yo, k, s1kp, sm]*repeat 45 times, k2tog, k, yo, k2, m1, k3, m1, sm, k3 (341)

13. K3, sm, m1, k3, m1, pm, *[k2tog, k, yo, k, yo, k, s1kp, sm]*repeat 47 times, m1, k3, m1, sm, k3 (345)

15. K3, sm, m1, k3, m1, k2, sm, *[k2tog, k, yo, k, yo, k, s1kp, sm]*repeat 47 times, k2, m1, k3, m1, sm, k3 (349)

17. K3, sm, m1, k3, m1, k, yo, k, s1kp, sm, *[k2tog, k, yo, k, yo, k, s1kp, sm]*repeat 47 times, k2tog, k, yo, k, m1, k3, m1, sm, k3 (353)

19. K3, sm, m1, k3, m1, k2tog, yo, k, yo, k, s1kp, sm, *[k2tog, k, yo, k, yo, k, s1kp, sm]*repeat 47 times, k2tog, k, yo, k, yo, s1kp, m1, k3, m1, sm, k3 (357)

21. K3, sm, m1, k3, m1, k, pm, *[k2tog, k, yo, k, yo, k, s1kp, sm]*repeat 49 times, k, m1, k3, m1, sm, k3 (361)

23. K3, sm, m1, k3, m1, yo, k, s1kp, sm, *[k2tog, k, yo, k, yo, k, s1kp, sm]*repeat 49 times, k2tog, k, yo, m1, k3, m1, sm, k3 (365)

25. K3, sm, m1, k3, m1, k2, yo, k, s1kp, sm, *[k2tog, k, yo, k, yo, k, s1kp, sm]*repeat 49 times, k2tog, k, yo, k2, m1, k3, m1, sm, k3 (369)

27. K3, sm, m1, k3, m1, pm *[k2tog, k, yo, k, yo, k, s1kp, sm]*repeat 51 times, m1, k3, m1, sm, k3 (373)

29. K3, sm, m1, k3, m1, k2, sm, *[k2tog, k, yo, k, yo, k, s1kp, sm]*repeat 51 times, k2, m1, k3, m1, sm, k3 (377)

31. K3, sm, m1, k3, m1, k, yo, k, s1kp, sm, *[k2tog, k, yo, k, yo, k, s1kp, sm]*repeat 51 times, k2tog, k, yo, k, m1, k3, m1, sm, k3 (381)

33. K3, sm, m1, k3, m1, k2tog, yo, k, yo, k, s1kp, sm, *[k2tog, k, yo, k, yo, k, s1kp, sm]*repeat 51 times, k2tog, k, yo, k, yo, s1kp, m1, k3, m1, sm, k3 (385)

35. K3, sm, m1, k3, m1, k, pm, *[k2tog, k, yo, k, yo, k, s1kp, sm]*repeat 53 times, k, m1, k3, m1, sm, k3 (389)

37. K3, sm, m1, k3, m1, yo, k, s1kp, sm, *[k2tog, k, yo, k, yo, k, s1kp, sm]*repeat 53 times, k2tog, k, yo, m1, k3, m1, sm, k3 (393)

39. K3, sm, m1, k3, m1, k2, yo, k, s1kp, sm, *[k2tog, k, yo, k, yo, k, s1kp, sm]*repeat 53 times, k2tog, k, yo, k2, m1, k3, m1, sm, k3 (397)

41. K3, sm, m1, k3, m1, pm, *[k2tog, k, yo, k, yo, k, s1kp, sm]*repeat 55 times, m1, k3, m1, sm, k3 (401)

42. Knit all.

Bind off loosely. Wet block the shawl into a half-moon shape overnight. When dry, you may press lightly with a warm iron if you wish. Weave in ends.

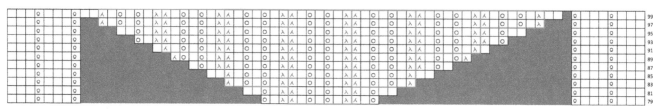

Symbols

☐	knit	λ	s1kp
O	yo	Q	m1
λ	k2tog	▓	no stitch

Snickerdoodles

This childhood favorite is known for its cinnamon sugar coating and crinkled top. You know you've baked them perfectly when each cookie is crispy and soft at the same time. For added fun for a specific party theme, you can color the dough with food coloring.

Makes 2 1/2 dozen cookies

For the cookies:
2 cups (400g) granulated sugar
1 1/4 cups (275g) salted butter (if using
    unsalted, add 1/4 teaspoon salt to the dry
    ingredients)
3/4 cup (175ml) vegetable oil
3 eggs
1 1/2 teaspoons vanilla extract
4 1/2 cups (540g) all-purpose flour
2 3/4 teaspoons cream of tartar
1 3/4 teaspoons baking soda

For the topping:
6 tablespoons ground cinnamon
6 tablespoons granulated sugar

1. Cream the sugar and butter together until light and fluffy. Add the oil, eggs, and vanilla, mixing the ingredients together well after each one is added.

2. In a separate bowl, mix the flour, cream of tartar, and baking soda together. Add to the wet ingredients and stir until thoroughly combined. Chill the dough for 30–60 minutes.

3. Meanwhile, mix the cinnamon and sugar together in a shallow dish. Set aside.

4. Preheat the oven to 350°F (180°C).

5. Form golf ball-sized balls of dough and roll them in the dish of cinnamon sugar. Bake on an ungreased cookie sheet for 10 minutes, until the edges are light brown. You want them to be chewy and soft in the middle with a light, crispy texture at the edges.

6. Transfer the cookies to a wire rack and let them sit until cool, then place on a serving dish or in an airtight storage container.

Smudge's Handspun Headband

Handspun wool yarn is like a raw gemstone tumbled and refined to shine and sparkle. Anything created with something so beautiful needs to be simple enough to let the yarn be the hero. I designed this headband with that in mind. Sara of Smudge Yarns dyed and spun this from the wool of local Irish sheep.

Materials:
40–50yd / 36–46m / 16g handspun knitting yarn in DK weight.
I used Smudge Yarns.

Tools:
5.5mm / US9 circular knitting needles or size needed to obtain gauge
Scissors and needle to weave in ends.

Pattern Gauge:
8sts x 14rows = 2in x 2in, in pattern

Finished Size:
Adult

Special Instructions:
All slipped stitches done purlwise with yarn at back

CO 85 stitches with long-tail cast on

Slip last stitch to other needle, place stitch marker on needle where last stitch was and K2tog to join in the round leaving 84 stitches on needles and marker showing beginning/end of round.

Row 1: K1, slip 1, K1, YO, PSSO last two stitches, *K2, sl1, K1, yo, PSSO last two sts* repeat to end of row

Row 2: Knit all until 12 stitches remain in row then wrap and turn

Row 3: *sl 1, K1, YO, PSSO last two stitches, K2* repeat until 12 stitches remain in the row. Wrap and turn

Row 4: Purl all but leave the last 12 stitches, wrap and turn

Row 5: *K2, sl1, K1, yo, PSSO last two sts* all around

Row 6: Knit all

Row 7: *sl 1, K1, YO, PSSO last two stitches, K2* repeat until 20 stitches remain in the row. Wrap and turn

Row 8: Purl all but leave the last 20 stitches, wrap and turn

Row 9: *K2, sl1, K1, yo, PSSO last two sts* all around

Row 10: Knit all

Row 11: *sl 1, K1, YO, PSSO last two stitches, K2* repeat until 12 stitches remain in the row. Wrap and turn

Row 12: Purl all but leave the last 12 stitches, wrap and turn

Row 13: *K2, sl1, K1, yo, PSSO last two sts* all around

Row 14: Knit all

Bind off and weave in ends

Block gently to retain stretchiness.

Summer

Aunt Nell's Blondies

I grew up hearing stories about my great Aunt Nell. From her generous heart to her skills in the kitchen, she was a bit of a legend in my mind as a child. Even now, I still marvel a bit. My Grandma, a self-proclaimed chocolate lover, especially loved this take on the traditional brownie bar.

1lb 5oz (600g) white chocolate
2/3 cup (150g) butter, at room temperature
3 eggs
1 1/4 cups (250g) light brown sugar
1 teaspoon vanilla extract
2 cups (240g) all-purpose flour
1 teaspoon baking soda
1/4 teaspoon salt

Makes 9 large squares

1. Preheat the oven to 325°F (160°C). Lightly grease a 9in x 9in (23cm x 23cm) square baking dish or line it with parchment paper.

2. Put the white chocolate and butter in a heatproof bowl set over a pot of simmering water (a double boiler), making sure the water does not touch the bottom of the bowl. Allow the chocolate and butter to melt, then remove from the heat and set aside to cool slightly.

3. In a large mixing bowl, beat the eggs, sugar, and vanilla extract together. Stir in the melted chocolate. In a separate bowl, whisk together the flour, baking soda and salt, then gently fold the flour mixture into the chocolate mixture until they are completely blended.

4. Pour the mixture into the prepared baking dish and bake for 40–50 minutes. The blondies are done when a knife inserted into the center comes out clean. Cool in the baking dish for at least 30 minutes before cutting into 9 large squares.

Mary's Hostess Apron

As a little girl, I loved wearing my Grandma's apron. I felt like it gave me magical baking powers. Of course, having Grandma with me was actually my magic. Years later, after many store-bought aprons, it is her original that still makes me smile to wear. So I measured and replicated it to share with you. It is a simple skirt with room for your style.

Materials:
   42in x 22in prewashed woven cotton
   fabric (main fabric)
   4 1/2 yd coordinating 1-inch wide bias
   tape
   4in x 30in inches prewashed coordinating
   woven cotton fabric (hem accent)
   Coordinating thread

Finished Size:
   Adult, 23in long

Tools:
   Sewing machine, sewing pins, scissors

1. **Pleats:** Spread the main fabric with the 42in length stretching left to right – the long edges will be the top and bottom of your apron. Measure to the center of fabric (21in is center). Moving out from the center, place outward-facing folds two inches from the center point on both sides. Pin one inch and two inches from the top edge of the fabric to secure. Repeat this twice more moving outwards from the two existing pinned folds, four inches apart each time.

2. **Waist:** Trim the bias tape to have an 80in length to work with for the waist. Center the middle point of the bias tape on so it folds over the center point of the just-pinned top of the apron. Pin into place. Proceed to pin the bias tape folded over the length of the top edge of the apron fabric. This will be the waist sash. Sew along the top to secure the bias tape to the apron fabric and stitch the pleats into place.

3. **Hem:** Turning focus to the bottom hem of the apron, place the hem accent fabric right-side facing the right side of the apron fabric. Pin together, leaving 1in for the seam. Stitch together closer to the pins than the fabric edges. Press with a warm iron, then on the right side, stitch along to secure the raw edge of the hem accent to the back of the apron fabric, while also adding a decorative stitch line to the front.

4. **Edging:** Pin the remaining bias tape around the remaining unfinished three edges of the apron and sew to secure.

5. **Finish:** Press the entire garment with a warm iron to finish the piece.

Buttery Cheddar Biscuits

After college, I moved back to my hometown and, in the midst of entering the real world, there was one weekly oasis of worry-free friend time – our Monday movie and picnic night. I usually made something for our potluck meal, but it was my cheddar biscuits that were the consistent favorite. To this day, they're the items I toss in a picnic or bread basket to accompany a meal.

For the biscuits:
2 cups (240g) self-rising flour
2 teaspoons baking powder
1 teaspoon salt
3/4 teaspoon paprika
1 tablespoon granulated sugar
1 1/4 cups (125g) grated mature Cheddar
3/4 cup (175ml) plain yogurt
2 tablespoons whole milk
3/4 teaspoon cream of tartar
1/2 cup (75g) sundried tomatoes, cut into
     thin slivers (optional)
1/2 cup (110g) butter, chilled and cubed

Makes 12 biscuits

For the topping:
1 egg white
2 tablespoons milk
1/4 teaspoon paprika
sea salt
1/4 cup (25g) grated mature cheddar

1. Preheat the oven to 475°F (245°C). Grease a baking sheet.

2. Sift together the flour, baking powder, salt, and paprika, then sprinkle in the sugar. Stir in the grated cheese.

3. In a separate large bowl, blend the yogurt and milk together with the cream of tartar. Stir in the dry ingredients bit by bit, blending with a wooden spoon. Stir in the sundried tomatoes. When it resembles dough, cut in the butter. Work the dough gently and quickly to avoid overworking or warming it. Do not overwork the dough; handle it as little as possible as to not melt the butter with your hands.

4. Pat the dough into a large flat circle and cut it into 8 triangular sections, or cut into circles with a scone cutter or the rim of a drinking glass. Transfer to the greased baking sheet.

5. In a small bowl, lightly beat the egg white and milk together. Brush the tops of the biscuits with this egg wash (do not brush the sides), then sprinkle a little paprika, sea salt, and grated cheese on each one. Bake for 10–12 minutes, until the tops are light golden brown. Serve slightly warm or cold with butter.

On the Green Picnic Mat

A picnic can happen any time and any where, it only takes an attitude and a place to sit. This portable and washable picnic blanket can make a picnic anywhere – whether on a sunny beach or in a living room on a rainy day. The oilcloth backing protects you and your picnic against any moisture from the ground, making it ideal for more al fresco dining locations.

Materials:
1 square yard or meter prewashed oilcloth
1 square yard or meter prewashed and ironed cotton, trimmed to be two inches smaller on each side than the oilcloth
Coordinating thread

Tools:
Leather- or denim-specific sewing machine needle recommended

Finished Size:
One square yard or meter, depending on your fabric size.

1. Lay the two fabrics down on a large surface or open floor space. Place the right side of the oilcloth against the floor and lay the cotton fabric on top. Center the cotton with the right side facing up and two inches of the back of the oilcloth showing on each side.

2. Fold the edges of the oilcloth to cover the edge of the cotton with two inches oilcloth border on all sides. Pin into place.

3. For the corners, fold straight on two sides then fold the other two sides up, tucking the corner fold inside. This is the thickest part of the edging so pin carefully so you hold the edges in place without needing to struggle later when sewing. Pinning on the outside of the blanket and not at the folded over edge of the oilcloth is recommended for this reason.

4. Sew around all the oilcloth edges. Use a strong sewing machine needle and do not pull the fabric through, just let the foot progress the fabric for you. If there is a wrinkle or crease, don't worry, this is to sit on not to hang on the wall, imperfections add to the homemade element.

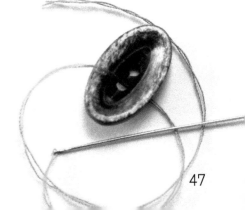

Lemon Drizzle Cake

My friend Molly loves lemon cake! Until I met her, I had nearly forgotten how to bake with lemons because I love their fresh flavors so much they'd rarely make it past being juiced. She reminded me of the tangy sweetness brought out with other ingredients in a lemon cake and I've been hooked ever since.

For the cake:
1 cup (120g) self-rising flour
1 cup (200g) granulated sugar
1/2 cup (110g) butter, at room temperature
1/4 cup (25g) ground almonds
2 eggs
grated rind of 1 lemon
4 tablespoons milk
1/2 teaspoon lemon extract

For the lemon drizzle:
juice of 1 lemon
3 heaped tablespoons confectioner's sugar,
    sifted

Serves 6

You'll also need:
Bundt cake tin that is 7in (18cm) across and
    3 1/2in (9cm) deep (5-cup capacity)

1. Preheat the oven to 350°F (180°C). Grease and lightly flour a Bundt cake tin that is 7in (18cm) across and 3 1/2in (9cm) deep.

2. Place all the cake ingredients into a large mixing bowl and mix just until smooth. Pour the batter into the prepared cake tin and bake for 40–45 minutes. The cake is done when a skewer or knife inserted into the center of a section of cake comes out clean. Let the cake cool in the tin on a baking rack. Once the cake is cool, invert the tin over a serving plate for the cake to drop out.

3. To make the lemon drizzle, mix the lemon juice and confectioner's sugar together. Pour it over the cake and leave to cool completely. Serve at room temperature.

Princes Street Market Tote

Nearly every day, I visit the local farmers' market or grocery store for fresh ingredients. I would go through countless plastic bags at that rate and paper bags just don't hold up in rainy weather, which makes fabric totes the perfect solution. You can adapt the size of this bag to be deeper and narrower for baguettes or shallower and wider for loaves of bread.

Materials:
    Two 24in long x 5in wide pieces of prewashed and ironed fabric (straps)
    Two 30in long x 18in wide pieces of prewashed and ironed fabric (outside and lining)
    Coordinating thread

Tools:
    Pins
    Sewing machine
    Safety pin
    Drawstring threader or shoelace

1. Make the handles first. Two 24-inch long x 5-inch wide pieces of fabric. Fold lengthwise wrong side facing out. Pin along the open edge side at least a half-inch from the raw edges to leave room to sewing. Do this with both straps. Proceed with sewing along the open sides of both straps then turn them right side out. I use a drawstring threader or shoelace with a safety pin threaded through to the other end to achieve this.

2. Place the two large pieces of fabrics with right sides facing outward. Decide which is the top and bottom. Along the top, fold the fabrics in together twice and pin for the top edge. Fold the fabric over so the lining faces outward and meet the raw side edges. Draw your attention to the top pinned edge and evenly place one end of each strap facing upwards, tucking the raw end under the pinned edge and repinning it into place. Turn the project over carefully and repeat this on the other side.

3. Once the straps are pinned into place with the top edge, sew it together with one row of stitches at the edge of the fold and one row of stitches at the top edge, securing the lining to the outer fabric and the straps to the bag.

4. Next, fold the project with the lining fabric facing out and the three side edges lined up. Pin along all three sides. Once pinned, proceed by sewing the three pinned sides together. Remove all pins.

5. Refold the bag sideways and focus your attention on the bottom two corners of the bag. Pin them straight across to create a stitched up triangle in each bag bottom corner. This helps the bag rest flat on the bottom to better prevent squashing of bread and produce.

Autumn

Orange and Honey Loaf Cake

This cake recipe is adapted from my great-grandmother's pound cake recipe. It is a perennial favorite with my family and a quick bake to make if you're having friends over for tea or hosting a casual tea-themed party. It is a cake that impresses in spite of being sublimely simple to make.

3/4 cup (175ml) milk
1/2 cup (110g) butter
1 cup (250ml) local honey
4 eggs
1 cup (200g) granulated sugar
1 teaspoon orange extract
2 cups (240g) self-rising flour

whipped cream, to serve

Makes 2 loaves

1. Preheat the oven to 350°F (180°C).

2. Generously butter 2 loaf pans. Dust them lightly with flour and tap out the excess. Alternatively, you could line the pans with baking paper.

3. In a small saucepan, warm the milk and butter until the butter has melted. Stir in the honey, making sure it does not stick to the bottom of the pan.

4. In a large mixing bowl, lightly beat the eggs until they are frothy, then add the sugar. Stir the warm milk mixture into the eggs and add the orange extract. Gradually blend the flour into the batter just until it is smooth.

5. Pour the batter into the prepared loaf pans. Place in the oven and bake for 30 minutes, or until the cakes have a very light golden color and an inserted knife comes out clean.

6. Let the cakes cool completely in the pans, then turn them out onto a serving plate. Serve with freshly whipped cream and drizzle with local honey.

Honeycomb Tea Cosy

As a child, I discovered my dresser had become home to a colony of bees. I hated to disrupt them so I just didn't open that drawer. Eventually, my parents learned of my winged roommates and insisted we move the occupied drawer outside so the bees could find a new home. My love of bees remained -- because not one stung me, I thought we were friends.

Materials:
Noro Kureyon Worsted weight yarn
33yd / 30m / 15g (MC)
-and-
Smudge Yarns Aran weight yarn
34yd / 31m / 20g (CC)
-or-
Any combination of two Worsted or Aran weight yarns to obtain gauge.

Tools:
5.5mm (US 9) circular or double-pointed knitting needles or size to obtain gauge.
Stitch holder (if not using magic loop with circular needles)
Scissors and needle to weave in ends.

Pattern Gauge:
The sample was knit at 14sts x 36rows / 4in x 4in garter stitch, blocked.

Finished Size:
Blocked cosy takes on size of teapot on which it is blocked. Can stretch up to 18in circumference at base of teapot and 8in top to bottom.

Notes:
All slipped stitches are slipped purlwise with yarn on wrong side
Carry MC up behind CC rows a few stitches in from the edge

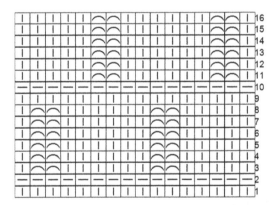

Symbols
| knit
— purl
⌒ slip

CO 64 stitches using long tail cast on with MC. Do not join.

Row 1: Use MC: Knit all, then join in the round

Row 2: Use MC: Purl all

Rows 3-8: Use CC: K5, sl 2 *K6, sl 2* K1

Row 9: Use MC: Knit all

Row 10: Use MC: Purl all

Row 11-12: Use CC: K1, sl 2 *K6, sl 2* K5

Work rows 13 through 32 over the first 32 stitches as follows. Place the remaining stitches on an extra needle, stitch holder, or let rest while implementing Magic Loop method.

Row 1 3: K5, sl 2 *K6, sl 2* K1

Row 14: P1, sl 2 *P6, sl2* P5

Row 15: K5, sl 2 *K6, sl 2* K1

Row 16: P1, sl 2 *P6, sl2* P5

Row 17-18: Use MC: Knit all

Row 19: Use CC: K1, sl 2 *K6, sl 2* K5

Row 20: P5, sl 2 *P6, sl 2* P1

Row 21: K1, sl 2 *K6, sl 2* K5

Row 22: P5, sl 2 *P6, sl 2* P1

Row 23: K1, sl 2 *K6, sl 2* K5

Row 24: P5, sl 2 *P6, sl 2* P1

Row 25-26: Use MC: Knit all

Row 27: Use CC: K5, sl 2 *K6, sl 2* K1

Row 28: P1, sl 2 *P6, sl2* P5

Row 29: K5, sl 2 *K6, sl 2* K1

Row 30: P1, sl 2 *P6, sl2* P5

Row 31: K5, sl 2 *K6, sl 2* K1

Row 32: P1, sl 2 *P6, sl2* P5

Break yarn. Place stitches on extra needle or holder. Repeat rows 13-32 with the other half of the stitches, but do not break the yarn at the end.

Row 33: Use MC: Knit all and reconnect both sets of stitches in the round

Row 34: Use MC: Purl all

Row 35–40: Use CC: K1, sl 2 *K6, sl 2* K5

Row 41: Use MC: Knit all

Row 42: Use MC: Purl all

Decrease rounds

Row 43: Use CC: *K2tog, K2tog, K2tog, sl2*, 40 stitches remain

Row 44–46: *K3, sl2*

Row 47: Use MC: Knit all

Row 48: Use MC: Purl all

Row 49-51: Use CC: k1, k2tog, s1, *k2tog, k2tog, s1*, to last st. Knit this st together with first stitch of next round, 24 stitches remain.

Row 52: k1, *s1, k2*, s1, k1

Row 53: With MC, knit

Row 54: Purl

Row 55: With CC, *k2tog, k1*, 16 stitches remain

Row 56: Purl. Break yarn.

Row 57: With MC, k1, *k2tog, k1*, 11 stitches remain.

Row 58: Purl. Cut the yarn you are working with, leaving ten inches, then thread it through the remaining stitches. Tie off loosely and weave in the remaining end.

For added finish, you may add a single crochet edge around spout and handle openings.

Weave in all ends. Wet block (place a tea towel around your teapot then place the damp tea cosy over it for blocking). Set in warm dry place. Change the tea towel each day until the tea cosy is completely dry. Sew on optional bee accents or bee buttons to finish the cosy design.

Monster Cookies

One of my college friends showed up with these flavorful cookies one day. Free cookies to a college student are appealing enough, but these had a multitude of flavors and textures that compelled me to eat quite a few. She even shared her mother's recipe, which I've adapted over the years to be what you see here today.

3 eggs
1 tablespoon baking soda
3/4 teaspoon vanilla extract
3/4 cup (120g) light brown sugar
1/2 cup (100g) granulated sugar
1/3 cup (75g) butter, softened
3 cups (200g) quick-cook oats
1 cup (225g) smooth peanut butter
3/4 cup (150g) plain M&Ms
1/4 cup (50g) semi-sweet or bittersweet
   chocolate chips

Makes 2 dozen cookies

1. Preheat the oven to 350°F (180°C). Lightly grease two baking sheets.

2. In a medium-sized mixing bowl, lightly beat the eggs, then stir in the baking soda and vanilla extract. Set aside.

3. In a large bowl, cream the sugars and butter together, then stir in the oats and peanut butter. Fold in the egg mixture. Sprinkle the M&Ms and chocolate chips on top and fold into the cookie dough.

4. Form golf ball-sized balls of cookie dough and place on the greased baking sheets. Flatten each ball slightly with the back of a large spoon or the palm of your hand. Leave at least 2in (5cm) between the cookies to give them room to expand when baking.

5. Bake for 8–10 minutes, until the edges are firm and lightly browned. Let them cool on the trays for 5 minutes before transferring to a wire rack. Once they are completely cool, store in an airtight container in a cool, dry place for up to 5 days.

Festive Bunting

I love how bunting adds a festive atmosphere to any space, but folds flat for storage – Not that I ever take mine down. This project works equally well with any woven cotton, whether it is an upcycled sheet or new lovely print quilt fabric. You could even make bunting using all the remaining fat quarters you want to use up for a vibrant and varied result.

Materials:
    4 half-yards of coordinating fabrics
    2 yards coordinating bias tape
    Coordinating thread for sewing

Tools:
    Sewing machine
    Scissors

Finished Size:
    6.5in wide at top x 8in from top to point

1. Photocopy the template on the next page and trim around the triangle border to create your pattern template. Place the template on your fabric and cut with straight fabric scissors. You will end up with a nice stack of triangles. If you are in a rush to decorate for a party or occasion then one-sided bunting is a good choice, use pinking shears to trim the triangles and skip the edge sewing (step 2).

2. Place two triangles together wrong-side facing one another and pin in place. Sew around the two pointed sides. Do this with all the triangles until you are done.

3. Leaving six inches at the end for tying, introduce the bias tape to the triangles starting at one end. Fold the bias tape over the straight top edge of each triangle and pin into place, leaving room to sew. Leave 2–4in between each triangle along the bias tape. Once all are pinned into place, it is time to sew them into a strand.

4. Using coordinating thread, sew the bias tape so it secures the various triangles into a strand of bunting. If using multiple fabrics, try to alternate colors and prints for visual appeal.

5. Press the bunting with a warm iron before hanging for a fresh decorative appearance.

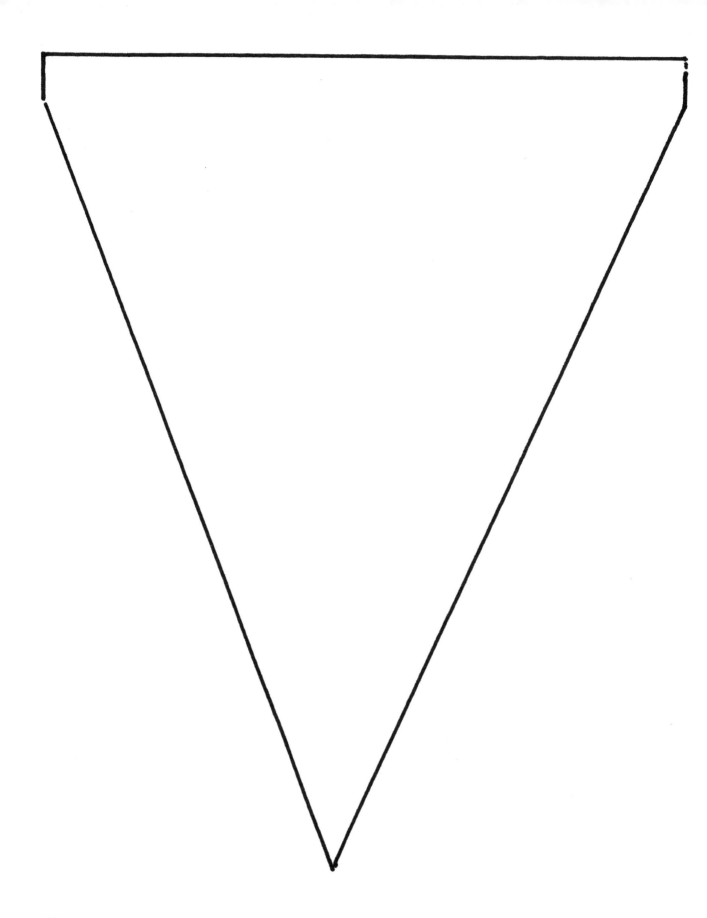

Grandma's Pumpkin Pie

The aroma of a homemade pumpkin pie is like a time travel portal leading back to every Thanksgiving and Christmas with my family. One Thanksgiving, we all were fighting a head cold so we had cheesy baked potatoes and pie. Really, what else did we need?

1 x 9in (23cm) cinnamon-infused Snyder pie crust (page 1)
1 fresh pie pumpkin, measuring 6–8in (15–20cm) across
2 eggs, separated
1 1/4 cups (250g) granulated sugar
1 tablespoon (15g) melted butter
3/4 teaspoon ground cinnamon, plus extra to decorate
1/4 teaspoon ground cloves
1 1/3 cups (325ml) whole milk (or half milk, half cream)
1 1/2 teaspoons brandy (optional)
confectioner's sugar, to decorate

Makes 1 x 9in (23cm) pie for 8 slices

1. Preheat the oven to 350°F (180°C) for the pie crust and pumpkin baking. Blind bake the pie crust according to the instructions on page 1.

2. Wash the outside of the pumpkin, then cut it in half with a serrated knife, like a bread or pumpkin knife. Using a metal ice cream scoop or large melon-baller, remove the seeds and stringy membranes. Place the pumpkin cut side down in a baking dish, cover with aluminum foil or a lid, and bake for 1 hour, or until the pumpkin is tender when poked with a fork. Let it cool until it is no longer steaming, then peel off the skin. Drain away excess water, then purée the pumpkin in a blender. At this point you can transfer it to an airtight container and freeze it until you are ready to make your pie or you can proceed to step 3.

3. Lower the oven temperature to 325°F (160°C) for the pie to be baked.

4. Measure out 1 1/3 cups (300g) of the pumpkin purée in a large bowl with plenty of mixing room. Mix in the egg yolks, sugar, melted butter, cinnamon, and cloves. Blend completely. Scald the milk, then stir it into the pumpkin mixture.

5. Beat the egg whites until they are fairly stiff, then fold into the pumpkin mixture. Taste the filling to make sure it is just a little too sweet. If not, add 1/4–1/2 cup (50–100g) more sugar and stir well. The pumpkin will absorb the sweetness, so if it is a little too sweet now, it will be perfectly sweetened once it is baked. If you'd like a little brandy flavor in your pie, this is the time to add it.

6. Set the pie dish on a baking sheet, then pour the pie filling into the cooled crust. Fill the crust as full as you can because the pie will shrink when cold. Place on the center rack in the oven. Bake for 10 minutes, then reduce the temperature to 325°F (160°C) and bake for 1 hour 15 minutes, until the filling is set and delicately browned.

7. Once done, dust with confectioner's sugar and a dash of cinnamon, then chill until ready to serve. Slice only when serving, not while hot.

Sugar Maple Vest

On chilly days when I don't feel like ironing, there is nothing better than a handknit sweater-vest. It helps what would otherwise be an ordinary pairing of tee shirt and jeans become a forcefield against brutal weather and a fashion statement in your favorite color. For this, I chose the natural Irish Aran wool that kept its sheep warm until shearing time.

Materials:
Smudge Wools Irish Aran weight yarn or similar yarn to obtain gauge
963yd / 880m / 566g
2 small buttons, 6 large buttons

Tools:
5.5mm (US 9) circular needles (though knit flat), or size needed to obtain gauge.
3 stitch holders or spare thread to hold them
Stitch markers
Scissors and needle to weave in ends.

Pattern Gauge:
The sample was knit at 14sts x 29rows / 4in x 4in garter stitch, blocked.

Finished Size:
Adult
22in from side-to-side,
24in from hem to base of cowl,
23in cowl circumference.

Loosely CO 90 sts
Rows 1–7: [K1, P1] repeat for all sts in these rows
Row 8: K6, Bind off 2, K74, Bind off 2, K6 (these will be buttonholes)
Row 9: K6, CO 2, K74, CO 2, K6
Rows 10–28: Knit all
Row 29: K6, Bind off 2, K74, Bind off 2, K6 (these will be buttonholes)
Row 30: K6, CO 2, K74, CO 2, K6
Rows 31–49: Knit all
Row 50: K6, Bind off 2, K74, Bind off 2, K6 (these will be buttonholes)
Row 51: K6, CO 2, K74, CO 2, K6
Rows 52–150: Knit all

For the neck section, you will be placing three sections on stitch holders, setting aside the current skein for a moment and working from two ends of a new skein. When starting with the ends of a new skein, leave six inches to weave in later.
Row 151: Place first 2 sts on Ha, K 41 (with one end of a new skein), place 4 sts on Hb, K 41 (with the other end of the new skein), place last 2 sts on Hc.
Row 152: Ignore the sts on holders and knit the two sections currently being worked with their respective skeins.
Row 153: Add 2 sts to Ha, K 37, place 2 sts from one side on Hb and 2sts from the other side on Hb, K 37, place 2 sts on Hc.
Row 154: Ignore the sts on holders and knit the two sections currently being worked with their respective skeins.
Row 155: Add 2 sts to Ha, K 33, place 2 sts from one side on Hb and 2sts from the other side on Hb, K 33, place 2 sts on Hc
Row 156: Ignore the sts on holders and knit the two sections currently being worked with their respective skeins.
Row 157: Add 2 sts to Ha, K 29, place 2 sts from one side on Hb and 2sts from the other side on Hb, K 29, place 2 sts on Hc
Row 158: Ignore the sts on holders and knit the two sections currently being worked with their respective skeins.

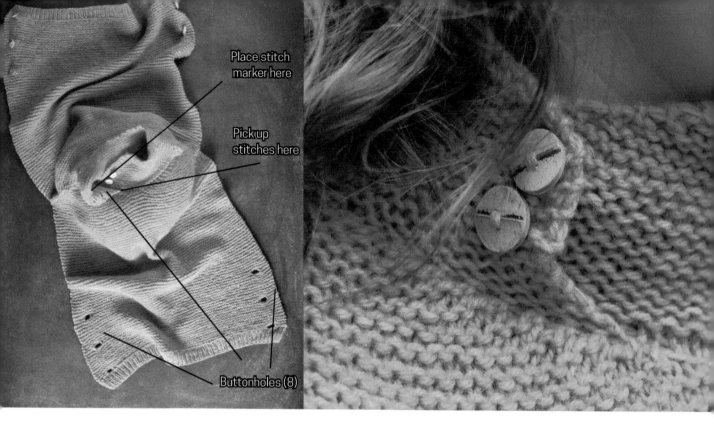

Place stitch marker here

Pick up stitches here

Buttonholes (8)

Row 159: Add 2 sts to Ha, K 25, place 2 sts from one side on Hb and 2sts from the other side on Hb, K 25, place 2 sts on Hc

Row 160: Ignore the sts on holders and knit the two sections currently being worked with their respective skeins.

Row 161: Add 2 sts to Ha, K 21, place 2 sts from one side on Hb and 2sts from the other side on Hb, K 21, place 2 sts on Hc

Row 162: Ignore the sts on holders and knit the two sections currently being worked with their respective skeins.

Row 163: Add 2 sts to Ha, K 17, place 2 sts from one side on Hb and 2sts from the other side on Hb, K 17, place 2 sts on Hc

Row 164: Ignore the sts on holders and knit the two sections currently being worked with their respective skeins.

Row 165: Add 2 sts to Ha, K 13, place 2 sts from one side on Hb and 2sts from the other side on Hb, K 13, place 2 sts on Hc

Row 166: Ignore the sts on holders and knit the two sections currently being worked with their respective skeins.

Row 167: Add 1 st to Ha, K 10, place 2 sts from one side on Hb and 2sts from the other side on Hb, K 10, place 1 st on Hc

Row 168: Ignore the sts on holders and knit the two sections currently being worked with their respective skeins.

Row 169: Add 1 st to Ha, K 7, place 2 sts from one side on Hb and 2sts from the other side on Hb, K 7, place 1 st on Hc

Row 170: Ignore the sts on holders and knit the two sections currently being worked with their respective skeins.

Row 171: Add 1 st to Ha, K 4, place 2 sts from one side on Hb and 2sts from the other side on Hb, K 4, place 1 st on Hc

Row 172: Ignore the sts on holders and knit the two sections currently being worked with their respective skeins.

Row 173: Add 1 st to Ha, K 3, ignore Hb sts, K 3, place 1 st on Hc

Row 174: Ignore the sts on holders and knit the two sections currently being worked with their respective skeins.

175 Row 173: Add 1 st to Ha, K 2, ignore Hb sts, K 2, place 1 st on Hc

176 Row 174: Ignore the sts on holders and knit the two sections currently being worked with their respective skeins.

177 Row 173: Add 1 st to Ha, K 1, ignore Hb sts, K 1, place 1 st on Hc

178 Row 174: Ignore the sts on holders and knit the two sections currently being worked with their respective skeins.

You should currently have 22 stitches each on Ha and Hc, and 44 stitches on Hb.

70

179 Row 175: K 1 st from Ha, K 1, ignore Hb until Cowl is worked, K 1, K 1 from Hc
180 Row 176: Ignore the sts on holders and knit the two sections currently being worked with their respective skeins.
181 Row 177: K 1 st from Ha, K 2, K 2, K 1 st from Hc
182 Row 178: Ignore the sts on holders and knit the two sections currently being worked with their respective skeins.
182 Row 179: K 1 st from Ha, K 3, CO 44 sts, K 3, K 1 st from Hc.
183 K 50
184 Row 180: K 1 st from Ha, K 50, K 1 st from Hc
185 Row 181: K 52
186 Row 182: K 1 st from Ha, K 52, K 1 st from Hc
187 Row 183: K 54
188 Row 184: K 1 st from Ha, K 56, K 1 st from Hc
189 Row 185: K 58
190 Row 186: K 2 st from Ha, K 58, K 2 st from Hc
191 Row 189: K 62

192 Row 190: K 2 sts from Ha, K 62, K 2 sts from Hc
193 Row 191: K 66
194 Row 192: K 2 sts from Ha, K 66, K 2 sts from Hc
195 Row 193: K 70
196 Row 194: K 2 sts from Ha, K 70, K 2 sts from Hc
197 Row 195: K 74
198 Row 196: K 2 sts from Ha, K 74, K 2 sts from Hc
199 Row 197: K 78
200 Row 198: K 2 sts from Ha, K 78, K 2 sts from Hc
201 Row 199: K 82
202 Row 200: K 2 sts from Ha, K 82, K 2 sts from Hc
203 Row 201: K 86
204 Row 202: K remaining 2 sts from Ha, K 86, K remaining 2 sts from Hc
205 Row 203: K 90

Rows 206–348: Knit all.
Rows 349–355: [K1, P1] repeat for all sts in these rows.

----------- cowl --------------
Place a stitch marker on your circular needles then transfer the 44 stitches from Hb onto the circular needle, working counter-clockwise (from the right shoulder, around the front of the garment to the back then to the right shoulder once more). You will pick up 8 along the right side of the neck, 44 from the cast on at the back, 8 from the left side of the neck. At this point, you will have returned to the stitch marker. You want 104 sts on your circular needles. The stitch marker will be at the other end of your stitches when you proceed to pick up 12 stitches from the row before the one on your needles, starting at the stitch marker and going towards the front center of the cowl neck. This will create an overlap swirl to the cowl and allow the buttons to match up. You will now have 116 stitches on your needles and may proceed with the knitting of the cowl.

Cowl Row 1–10: Slip the first stitch, K115
Cowl Row 11: Slip the first stitch, K2, Bind off 2, K111 (this will be a buttonhole)
Cowl Row 12: Slip the first stitch, K110, CO 2, K3
Cowl Rows 13–16: Slip the first stitch, K115
Cowl Row 17: Slip the first stitch, K2, Bind off 2, K111 (this will be a buttonhole)
Cowl Row 18: Slip the first stitch, K110, CO 2, K3
Cowl Rows 19–20: Slip the first stitch, K115
Cowl Rows 21–32: Slip the first stitch, K2tog, K1, K2tog, Knit until 5 stitches from end, K2tog, K1, K2tog

Bind off the remaining 68 stitches using Icelandic Bind-off (page 5).
Finish: Weave in ends. Sew on buttons to inside of back lined up with buttonholes on front sides and cowl collar.

Chocolate Cardamom Tart

Desserts don't always need to be sweet and this tart is proof. Even with a cup of sugar, the cocoa and cardamom balance the sweetness with a pleasant chocolate flavor. I recommend using a traditional pie crust, but feel free to make this your own with a crushed cookie crust if you prefer.

1 x 9in (23cm) cardamom-infused Snyder pie crust (page 1)
1 1/2 cups (375ml) cream
1/3 cup (75ml) whole milk
1 cup (170g) light brown sugar
1/3 cup (40g) plus 1 tablespoon fine baking cocoa, sifted
2 tablespoons all-purpose flour
2 teaspoons ground cardamom
1/4 teaspoon salt
1 tablespoon (15g) butter, at room temperature
1 teaspoon vanilla extract
2 egg whites
4 tablespoons granulated sugar

Makes 1 x 9in (23cm) pie for 8 slices

1. Preheat the oven to 350°F (180°C). Blind bake the pie crust according to the instructions on page 1.

2. Warm the cream and milk in a large pot. When it is starting to simmer, mix in the brown sugar, sifted cocoa, flour, ground cardamom, and salt. Warm the ingredients over a low heat and stir regularly until the mixture thickens. Stir in the butter and vanilla extract. Once the ingredients have melted together, pour the warm chocolate mixture into the pie crust and let it cool slightly.

4. In a separate bowl, beat the egg whites to soft peaks, then fold in the granulated sugar. Fold the egg whites into the chocolate mixture. Gently pour the filling into the pie crust.

5. Bake for 10 minutes or until the center of the pie barely jiggles. Cool on a wire rack before serving. This tart can also be refrigerated and served chilled.

Upcycled Felt Mittens

Years ago, a friend and I were wishing for more projects for all the pretty wool sweaters we'd accidentally felted in the laundry. From that, the idea for these mittens developed. I prefer using cotton jersey for the lining, but for added warmth, feel free to use fleece while remembering you will need to adjust to a larger mitten size for its added bulkiness.

Materials:
1 felted sweater with ribbed cuffs/hem
30in w x 11in h prewashed cotton jersey
Thread coordinating with the jersey
7ft embroidery thread in coordinating color

Tools:
Scissors
Sewing machine
Sturdy embroidery needle

Finished Sizes: *hand width / wrist to fingertip*
Small: 3in / 9.5in
Medium: 3.75in / 9.75in
Large: 4.5in / 10.5in

Special Instructions:
Print the pattern template on page 72 at 100%. To ensure accuracy, you can measure the large size at the widest point to make sure it is just shy of 7in (175mm). You can also use your own hand as a size guide and create your own template, but the provided template makes it easier to make a pair of mittens as a gift.

1. Place the felted sweater right-side out on a flat surface. Leaving a half-inch seam allowance on all sides, trim around your desired sized mitten template with the wrist section being over the ribbed cuff or hem of the felted sweater. If it helps, you may wish to pin the template to the fabric to keep it from moving while you cut. The small size works nicely on a sleeve and cuff, but the large would likely need to be done with the main section of the garment. Repeat this process with the jersey fabric, having it face wrong-side out as you are placing the template and cutting.

2. Pin the jersey liners together and, using a sewing machine, sew around the entire edge, leaving less than a quarter-inch between the stitches and raw edges. Leaving the liners wrong-side out, place each in the middle of the appropriate felted mitten cutouts.

3. Pin the two mitten template halves together wrong-side, and the jersey lining within each and out of sight, begin using the Blanket Stitch (tutorial on page 7) to stitch all the way around the edges of the mittens with the coordinating embroidery thread. Pull tightly without puckering the felt to keep the winter chill out when the mittens will later be worn. It usually takes three lengths of embroidery thread the length of your arm span to sew one mitten.

4. Continue the Blanket Stitch to secure the jersey lining to the felted ribbed cuff all the way around on both mittens. Knot off the thread when done and weave through, then trim the excess thread.

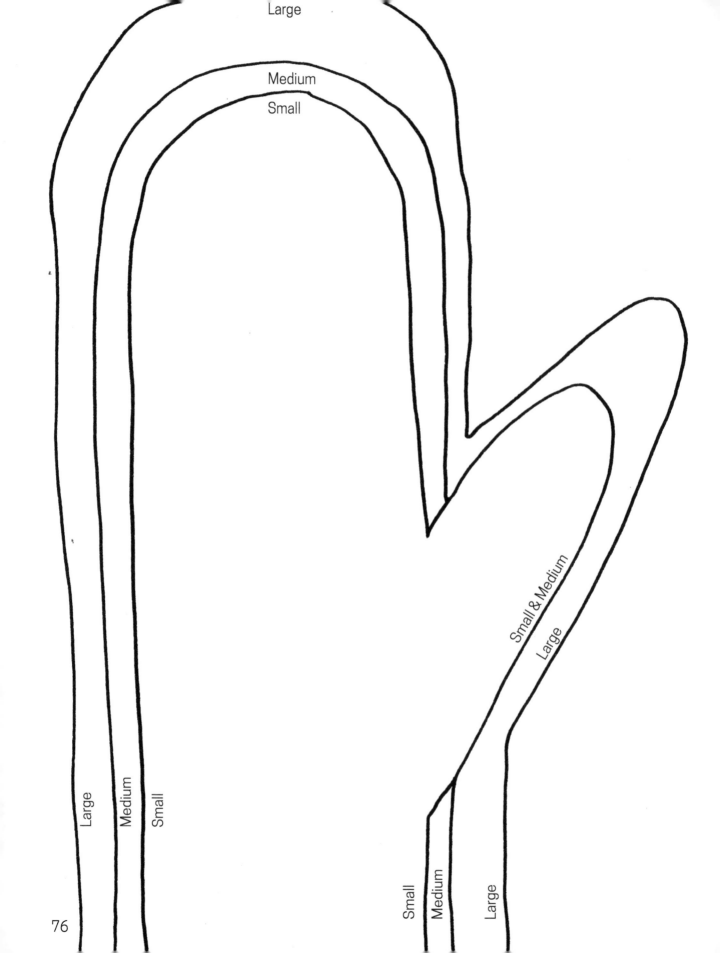

Large

Medium

Small

Large

Medium

Small

Small & Medium

Large

Small

Medium

Large

76

Acknowledgements

My Kickstarter backers and blog readers have fueled this book from the very beginning.
Thank you all for your enthusiasm and support. Especially grateful for my Sponsors:
    Ballymaloe Country Relish of Cork, Ireland
    Brochenn yarn shop of Landerneau, Bretagne, France
    BonnyAlma
    Campbell's Tea of Dublin, Ireland
    Nora Morris Kulkarni
    Dan O'Keeffe

This book was created with the expert help of a team of skilled professionals. Thank you all!
    Recipe Editor: Kristin Jensen
    Knitting Pattern Editor: Suzanne McEndoo
    Photographers: Fin McAteer (page 25) and Victor Sullivan (page 42)
    Model Stylist: Natasha Crowley
    Hair Stylist: Andrew Cronin
    Make-up Artist: Andrea Murphy
    Proofreaders: William G. Bail, Marseille Bunk, Arlene Cooke, Tim Nixon, Carlota Sage, and Victor Sullivan

My recipes wouldn't be worth a dash of salt without all the recipe testing that was done by volunteers.
    Thank you to the kitchen goddesses: Arlene Cooke, Sica Corey, Laura Natasha Hall,
    Máire Nobes, Julia Okenkova, Carlota Sage, Lorna Goodsell Walsh, and Sara Owen Willard.

My patterns were test knit by several skilled knitters. Thank you, 63Stella, BonnyAlma, Marseille Bunk,
    Kim Cullen, Liz DeVoss, Penny Ercolano, Siobhan Keane Hopcraft, Kathy Crooke Kyburz, M Beth Leath,
    Suzanne McEndoo, Carol O'Leary, Nuala McGrath, and Karen Simpson.

Thank you to the beautiful models: Maire O'Sullivan, Kate Lawlor, Arlene Cooke, and Hannah Fliesler.

The photographs of my designs benefited from beautiful County Cork, Ireland, backdrops:
    Camden Palace Hotel, Cork City
    Fish Bar at Electric, Cork City
    Griffins Garden Centre, Dipsey
    The English Market, Cork City
    Linehan's Design, Cork City
    North Main Street, Cork City
    The Princes Street Church
    St. Mary's Church, Cork City
    Triskel Christchurch, Cork City

Suppliers

Bake

Campbell's Tea
Perfect Tea since 1797
Dublin, Co. Dublin, Ireland
campbellstea.com

The English Market
Serving Cork since 1788
Cork City, Co. Cork, Ireland
englishmarket.ie

Knit

Dragonfly Fibers
Kensington, Maryland, USA
dragonflyfibers.com

Irish Fairytale Yarns
Cork, Co. Cork, Ireland
irishfairytaleyarns.com

Lucy Neatby
Nova Scotia, Canada
lucyneatby.com

Manos del Uruguay
Uruguay
manosyarns.com

Noro
Japan
noroyarns.com

Smudge Yarns
Co. Cork, Ireland
smudgeyarns.com

Sew

Cork Button Company
Buttons, Zippers, Thread, and Tailoring Supplies
Pope's Quay, Cork City, Co. Cork, Ireland
corkbuttoncompany.ie

Vibes & Scribes
Crafts, Wool, and Haberdashery
Bridge Street, Cork City, Co. Cork, Ireland
vibesandscribes.ie

Index